FUN-FILLED 5- to 10-MINUTE SCIENCE ACTIVITIES FOR YOUNG LEARNERS

200 Instant Kid-Pleasing Activities That Build Early Science Skills for Circle Time, Transition Time—or Any Time!

by Deborah Diffily

SCHOLASTIC
PROFESSIONAL BOOKS

NEW YORK   TORONTO   LONDON   AUCKLAND   SYDNEY
MEXICO CITY   NEW DELHI   HONG KONG   BUENOS AIRES

Cover and interior design by Josué Castilleja
Illustrations by Cary Pillo

ISBN 0-439-42056-3

7 8 9 10   40   09 08 07 06 05

TABLE OF CONTENTS

ABOUT THIS BOOK

Young children are natural scientists. They ask hundreds of questions, love to explore all kinds of materials, and will return to an activity that interests them again and again. When you think about it, these are the characteristics of professional scientists, too. Scientists ask questions and try to find the answers to those questions by exploring, experimenting, and repeating experiments. As early childhood educators, we nurture these natural tendencies in children and help create positive attitudes about science that will last a lifetime.

Many early childhood educators shy away from science, believing they do not know enough content to be a good science teacher. That is simply not true. To be an effective science teacher for young children, you simply adopt their curious attitude: ask questions, be willing to look for answers, explore, and experiment. The content knowledge you believe you should know can typically be learned from quality children's literature books about science topics. In the past few years, we've seen an increase in the number of science books that provide knowledge and background information at a read-aloud level that young children can easily understand. Dozens of these books are suggested. And, remember, you can learn right along with your students.

We already know that young children learn best through hands-on exploration and concrete learning experiences. This is particularly true for science. Some of the activities in this book are teacher demonstrations, but the vast majority are hands-on experiences for children. The activities introduce young children to different areas of science: life, physical, and earth science. However, the book itself is organized by science processes:

1. Observing

Of all the skills scientists rely on, observation is the one that is most often used. The same is true for young children. They can observe scientific things many times a day, but we have to help them move from simply seeing things to true observation. Basically, we want children to notice how things work, how things move, and how things change.

2. Sorting and Classifying

Objects can be sorted by the materials they are made of, their color, shape, size, and weight. While scientists sort organisms by very sophisticated characteristics, young children learn to sort things by very observable traits. Perhaps the simplest form of sorting is grouping boys and girls. Beyond that, boys and girls can be sorted by the color of their hair, the color of their eyes, the type of clothes they are wearing, and so on.

3. Asking Questions

Scientists spend their lives asking and answering questions. When children ask questions about the world around them, they begin to act like scientists. As adults, we do not have to know the answers to all their questions. Our role is to help children find different ways to answer science-related questions—through observation, reading a book, searching the Internet, or talking with experts.

4. Predicting

Scientists make predictions based on some kind of evidence or form of observation—just as the ones we ask children to make. Predictions should not just be guesses about what will happen. We can help young children understand how to use what they know to make a prediction by showing them the front cover of a book. Looking at the cover to predict what the book will be about is a simple form of using observation to predict.

5. Experimenting

This simply means trying out an idea to see what will happen. Scientists may explore more theoretical questions, but they follow the same procedures that you and your children will: asking a question, making a hypothesis, conducting an experiment, recording findings, and making conclusions. For children, simply observing the world and making predictions about what might happen often lead to experiments and investigations.

6. Measuring and Estimating

Scientists measure items at molecular levels and at galactic levels, and develop estimates for things at both ends of this huge continuum. Young children need to measure more concrete things. Luckily, opportunities for measurement surround them every day—in cooking, in trying on new shoes, in building projects, and so on.

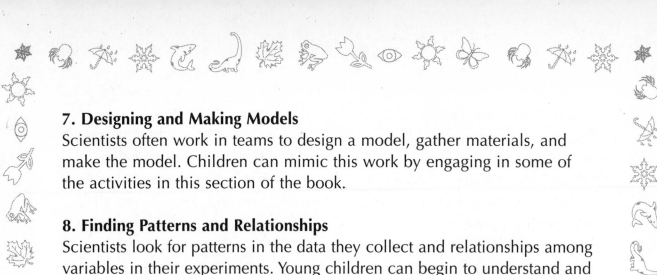

7. Designing and Making Models

Scientists often work in teams to design a model, gather materials, and make the model. Children can mimic this work by engaging in some of the activities in this section of the book.

8. Finding Patterns and Relationships

Scientists look for patterns in the data they collect and relationships among variables in their experiments. Young children can begin to understand and look for patterns and relationships in their own world. Patterns are every-where—in nature, in our homes, even in the clothes that we wear. We can also help children begin to see relationships, such as the relationship between the clothes they wear and the weather, and between the activities they do and the time of day.

9. Communicating

Scientists share what they learn by talking with colleagues and with other people who are interested in their work. Teach children to communicate in the same way. Scientists also record their observations, findings, and conclusions. Young children can do this by drawing, writing, or doing a combination of both.

Please note that the activities in this book do not support just one of the processes. Many learning experiences could be placed into two or more of the categories because, when you experiment, you simultaneously ask questions, make predictions, observe, and communicate.

In our early childhood classrooms, it seems that we have less time for science than in years past. Still, science is simply too important to ignore. This book focuses on learning experiences that can be accomplished in a few minutes of class time. Many of these activities can take more (or less) than 5 to 10 minutes. For example, when creating a K-W-L chart with your class (page 60), you could spend 10 minutes a day for five days working on the chart or you could extend the time each day to match the children's interest and attention span. The experiments and model-building activities can be accomplished in 10 minutes—only if all the materials are organized and ready for children.

Some activities, such as the balloon-race activity (page 50), may take 10 minutes to explore, followed by another 10 minutes to discuss what happened. Other activities, such as observing ants or mealworms (page 25), take only a moment but should be repeated over several days. Some of the activities are introduced to the whole group, then completed during independent study or center time—such as making BrainQuest® cards (page 26). Rather than choosing an activity because it lasts only 5 to 10 minutes, you should select an activity based on how it pertains to the class's learning. When planning these activities for use in your classroom, it is important to remember the limited attention span of young children and vary learning activities accordingly.

As you and your children explore some of these activities together, remember:

If a child is to keep alive his inborn sense of wonder, he needs the companionship of at least one adult who can share it... rediscovering with him the joy, excitement, and mystery of the world we live in.

—Rachel Carson, *The Sense of Wonder*

Enjoy the book!

OBSERVING

W Whole-group activity   **S** Small-group activity
I Individual activity   **T** Transition   **RA** Read-aloud

W Watching Candy Grow

Stir one cup of sugar into 1/2 cup of water until most of the sugar has dissolved. Heat the mixture on a hot plate, stirring until it boils. Stop stirring and let the mixture boil for one minute. Put a craft stick into a glass. Carefully pour the liquid into the glass and set it aside. Invite children to observe the glass and stick every day as "candy" grows on both the glass and the stick.

W Let It Rain!

When it rains for the first time in a long time, use the weather event as a teachable moment. Stop what you are doing for a few minutes and enjoy a few minutes of just watching it rain.

Reinforce children's observation of rain by reading *Down Comes the Rain* by Franklyn M. Branley (HarperTrophy, 1997).

W Let It Snow!

When snow is predicted, chill black construction paper in the freezer. Encourage children to catch falling snowflakes on the frozen paper and examine them with a magnifying glass. Or, when it snows for the first time in a long time, use the weather event as a teachable moment. Stop what you are doing and enjoy a few minutes of just watching it snow.

Read *Snow Is Falling* by Franklyn M. Branley (HarperCollins, 2000) to reinforce children's observation of snowfall.

W Shrinking Puddles

After a rainfall, take children outdoors and mark the edges of puddles. Return the next day to observe how much of the puddles has evaporated.

W Observing Habitats: Ponds

Take a quick field trip to a nearby pond and look for animal life in and around the pond.

Before the field trip, read *Pond Life (Cycles of Life)* by David Steward (Franklin Watts, 2002), and ask children to generate a list of what they expect to see at the pond. After the field trip, read *In the Small, Small Pond* by Denise Fleming (Henry Holt, 1998), and make a list of animals children observed at the pond.

W Observing Habitats: Meadows

Take a quick field trip to a nearby meadow and look for animal life in and around the meadow.

Before the field trip, read *How to Hide a Meadow Frog and Other Amphibians* by Ruth Heller (Grosset & Dunlap, 1995), and have children make a list of animals to look for in the meadow. After the field trip, read *In Fields and Meadows* by Tessa Paul (Crabtree, 1997), and list the animals children observed at the meadow.

W Life Cycles

Ask children to observe life cycles of organisms in their habitat—such as silkworms in mulberry leaves, tadpoles in pond water, or mealworms in oatmeal—over several days. Record the animals' growth stages on a class chart using children's input.

S Make Your Own Rainbow

Gather the following materials and place
them in a center: scissors, typing paper,
card stock, a ruler, masking tape, clear
glass, a flashlight, a chair, and water.

Have children trace the front of
the flashlight onto the card stock,
then cut a slit in that circle ending 1/2
inch from the edges. Tape the circle
on the front of the flashlight. Next,
ask children to fill the glass 3/4 full
of water and place it on the edge
of the chair. Have one child hold the
typing paper just above the floor near one leg of the chair. Darken the
room slightly. Another child should hold the flashlight at an angle to the
water level. Later, ask children to record their findings by drawing what
they saw with crayons or colored pencils.

S Make Your Own Rainbow Outside

During a warm, sunny day, get a garden hose with a sprayer attached
and a source of running water. Adjust the sprayer nozzle so that the hose
produces a fine spray. Encourage children to experiment holding the hose in
different positions to make a rainbow, then discuss their findings. (Note: A
rainbow can be seen only when the sun is behind the person and the spray).

W Fossilize a Sponge

Show how a fossil is formed with the following experiment: Cut a sponge
into a bone shape (keep the rest of the sponge for comparison). Stir Epsom
salt into a cup of hot water until no more salt will dissolve. Add a few drops
of food coloring, then pour the liquid into a shallow pan. Place the sponge
in the liquid, then set it aside in a place where it will not be moved. Invite
children to observe the sponge for a few minutes each day until the sponge
is completely dry. Have them look closely at the holes in the sponge. This
activity demonstrates how minerals attach to the sides of holes in bones,
seashells, or plants and create a fossil.

S Insect Dominoes

Before asking children to observe live insects, invite them to play a game of Insect Dominoes. Photocopy "Insect Dominoes" (page 16) on card stock. Cut apart the dominoes along the dashed lines and store the dominoes in resealable bags. Point out the obvious characteristics that differentiate insects from other small creatures—six legs and three body parts. Review the game rules, then post the following instructions:

Turn all dominoes facedown in a pile. Each player selects five dominoes. Turn over one domino. Players take turns matching one side of a domino in play. If a player cannot make a match, he or she must take a domino from the pile. The game is over when one player plays all of his or her dominoes.

S Cracking Rocks

Collect several rocks that have cracks in them. Put the rocks in the freezer in individual containers of water. When the water is frozen, have small groups of children carefully break each "iced rock" with a hammer. Have children observe how they break (for example, easily or evenly) and make connections between their small experiment and nature's force on rocks.

I Noticing the Little Things

Have children draw a self-portrait. Several days later, set up a mirror and ask children to draw another self-portrait as they observe themselves in the mirror. Encourage them to use their observational skills to sketch in details such as the shape of their eyes and lips, and the way their hair falls (or does not fall) on their foreheads. Compare the two self-portraits and discuss how careful observation helps them create a more detailed drawing.

I Looking at Leaves

Have children collect leaves and observe the leaf parts through hand lenses. Ask them to describe what they observe.

① Mining for Ore

Fill a plastic container half full of clean sand. Stir in a large quantity of iron filings and several objects that will not be attracted to a magnet. Have individual children use a magnetic wand to pull the filings out of the sand. Ask children to hide the filings again when they are finished exploring. After every child has had an opportunity to "mine for ore," lead a discussion about why the magnet attracted only the filings.

① Changing Colors

Put one spoonful of white paint in a small container, such as an empty film canister. Prepare one container for each child. Ask each child to add one drop of red, blue, or yellow paint to the container, stirring well with a paintbrush. Have each child record changes in the color by painting one brushstroke on paper after each successive drop of primary-colored paint. Ask them to describe the changes of hue they create.

Teaching Tip
Place primary-colored paint in a squirt bottle so that only one drop is released at a time.

① Grinding Corn

Place a mortar and pestle in a learning center with dried kernels of corn. Encourage children to take turns grinding the corn and observing the changes from kernel to cornmeal.

(T) I Spy

Model how to give a very detailed description of an item in the room and encourage children to guess what the item is after each hint. Ask one child to describe an item in the room and let other children guess. Challenge the child to give more and more details.

(T) I Am Thinking, You Are Guessing

Describe an animal by giving descriptive hints one at a time. Encourage children to guess the animal after each hint. For example, say "*I am thinking of an animal. It is a reptile. It comes from an egg. It has four legs. It has a very good way to defend itself against enemies. It moves slowly.*" Continue describing the animal until children guess the answer (*turtle*).

(RA) *Two Bad Ants*
by Chris Van Allsburg (Houghton Mifflin, 1988)

This story takes readers on an adventure exploring everything in the house as seen from the ants' point of view.

(RA) *Look Up, Look Down*
by Tana Hoban (Greenwillow, 1992)

Hoban's photographs illustrate how everyday objects look when viewed from above and below.

Try This! Provide each child with a paper-towel tube. Invite children to explore the classroom by viewing it through the restricted view of the tube. Discuss how objects seem different when viewed from this perspective.

RA Look! Look! Look!
by Tana Hoban (Greenwillow, 1988)

Hoban's delightful photographs fool the eye by first revealing only a small square of each photograph. Children have the opportunity to predict what is depicted.

Try This! Using a familiar picture book as a template, trim a piece of cardboard to the size of the book's page and cut out a small square. Place the cardboard over an illustration and ask children to guess from what book the illustration comes.

Try This, Too! Cover a picture of an animal or other science-related picture with a peephole viewer (see page 17). Open peephole windows one at a time and have children try to figure out what the picture is. After several experiences with this activity, place several laminated pictures and some peephole viewers in the science center for individuals or small groups to explore.

RA What Makes a Shadow?
by Clyde Bulla (HarperCollins, 1994)

In this book, the author uses children and animals to explain in simple terms what a shadow is and how it is created.

Try This! Set up a lamp in a darkened area of the classroom. Ask pairs of children to create shadows using their bodies and classroom materials. Encourage children to manipulate their shadows by changing the angle of the light or moving the objects so that the light hits them at different angles.

Try This, Too! Pair up children and give each pair several pieces of chalk. On a sunny day, take children outside and have them take turns tracing the outline of each other's shadow. To extend this activity, do it in the morning and again in the afternoon, and discuss why the shadows are in different places.

RA From Seed to Plant
by Gail Gibbons (Holiday House, 1993)

Gibbons uses simple language to explain how seeds become plants, then make new seeds.

Try This! Provide each child with a clear plastic cup, a cup of soil, and several radish seeds. Since these seeds grow very quickly, have children make an entry into individual journals every other day to record their observations of the radish plants as they grow.

RA Dandelions: Stars in the Grass
by Mia Posada (Carolrhoda Books/Lerner, 2000)

Posada uses rhyme to explain the life cycle of dandelions. She provides facts about dandelions, and even a recipe for dandelion salad.

Try This! Give each child a magnifying glass, observation log, and one or two dandelions. Ask them to observe the dandelions very carefully and sketch what they see. Later in the day, have children return to their dandelions and their drawings. Ask them to add more details. Pair children so that they can help each other see how they could make their drawings more detailed.

Insect Dominoes

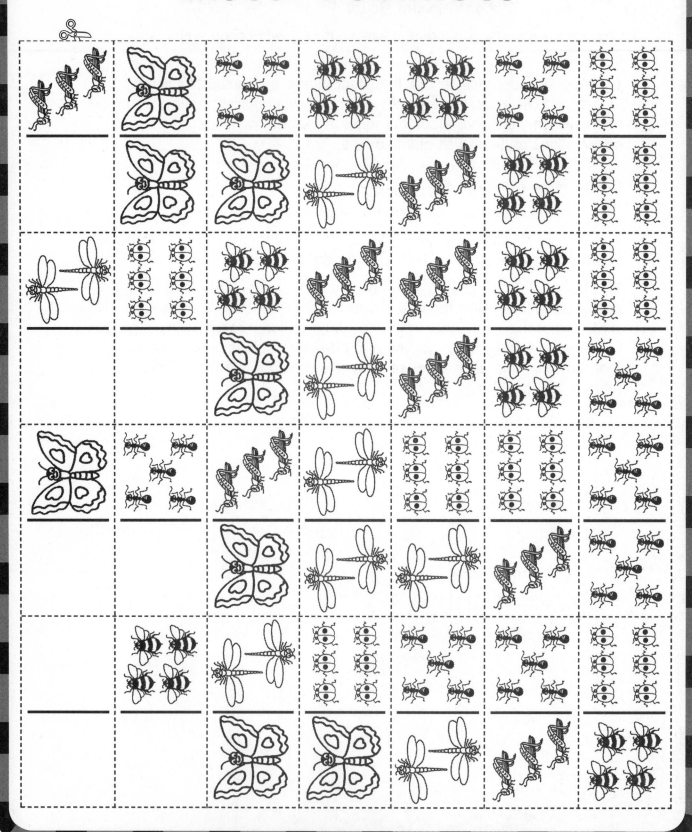

FUN-FILLED 5- TO 10-MINUTE SCIENCE ACTIVITIES FOR YOUNG LEARNERS

Peephole Viewer

Cut out the dashed lines.
Then fold at the solid line to open each window.

SORTING AND CLASSIFYING

W Whole-group activity   **S** Small-group activity

I Individual activity   **T** Transition   **RA** Read-aloud

W Recycle, Reuse!

Introduce the concept of recycling to children by putting a paper recycling bin in the classroom. Discuss what kinds of paper can be recycled. Ask children to be careful when they are cleaning the room and to always put recyclable paper in the recycling bin.

Read Gail Gibbons's *Recycle: A Handbook for Kids* (Little, Brown, 1996) to add to children's understanding of recycling and why it is important.

W How Many Kinds of Water?

Identify and describe bodies of water such as rivers, streams, lakes, ponds, and oceans. Ask children to locate photographs in nature magazines of different kinds of natural sources of water. Encourage children to create a bulletin board of bodies of water.

Extend children's discussion by reading *It Could Still Be a Lake* by Allan Fowler (Children's Press, 1997).

S Transportation

Provide a collection of small toy vehicles, such as motorcycles, cars, pick-up trucks, work-related trucks, and boats. Ask children to sort the collection and describe how they are sorting the vehicles.

T Walk Like an Animal

When ending one activity, ask children to move to a particular area of the room for the next activity by floating like a butterfly, scampering like a mouse, lumbering like an elephant, walking as slowly as a turtle, and so on.

(S) Seashell Sorting

Place a collection of seashells in a center. Encourage partners to sort the shells, then describe the characteristics they used for sorting.

For children who have difficulty with sorting seashells, begin with a simpler form of the activity. Provide a set of shells with one large shell and a small shell of the same type. Tell children to choose a small shell, then find the same shell in a larger size. Have them put the shells aside in a pair, then repeat until all the shells are in pairs.

(RA) *Out of the Ocean*
by Debra Frasier (Harcourt, 1998)

This story follows people walking along the edge of the water finding all kinds of treasure.

Try This! Bury several pairs of seashells in a sandbox (or plastic container half full of sand). Challenge children to find the pairs using only their sense of touch.

(I) Living or Not?

Divide a piece of paper into two columns and label one column "Living" and the other, "Nonliving." Make enough copies for each child and distribute them with a clipboard. Take a short walking field trip through the neighborhood or just out to the playground. Ask each child to write or draw things that they observe, putting each item in the correct column.

(I) Going Nuts

Set up a learning center with a basket containing 5 to 10 nuts from four or five varieties—pecans, walnuts, almonds, brazil nuts, peanuts. Include four or five smaller baskets or bowls in the center. Initially, ask children to simply sort the nuts. Then challenge children to predict which type of nut would be the hardest to open and which would be the easiest. When the interest in sorting nuts begins to wane, add a nutcracker to the center so children can test their predictions—and allow them to eat the nuts they crack. (Make sure to check for food allergies first.)

W Fruit or Vegetable?

Bring in vegetables that represent different parts of a plant: roots (potatoes, carrots), stems (celery, asparagus), leaves (lettuce, cabbage, spinach), and flowers (cauliflower, broccoli, artichokes). Likewise, provide a variety of fruits, making sure to include cucumbers, tomatoes, squash, or snow peas—all of which are considered fruits.

Sort the food you brought in by placing fruits on one table and vegetables on another. Ask children to describe the similarities and differences between the two groups, and record their observations on the board. Cut open the food and have children compare the foods again. Children should now be able to observe that one group has seeds and the other does not. Tell children that everything on one table are fruits and on the other, vegetables. Ask children to come up with their own definition of a fruit and vegetable.

To extend children's familiarity with different fruits and vegetables, introduce *Eating the Alphabet* by Lois Ehlert (Harcourt, 1993).

S Magic Magnets

Divide the class into small groups. Provide each group with a magnet and a resealable plastic bag containing many different objects. Ask children to sort the objects into two groups: those attracted to a magnet and those not attracted to a magnet.

After this first sort, give each group a cookie sheet and ask them to test the items in the group that is attracted to a magnet. Can the magnet move the item even when the cookie sheet is between them?

S Magnetic Shields

Extend the "Magic Magnets" activity above by having children test to see if a magnet can move paper clips when materials such as paper, glass, water, or wood are between them. Have children fill out "Is It a Shield for a Magnet?" (page 21) before they start experimenting.

RA *The Cloud Book*
by Tomie de Paola (Holiday House, 1985)

De Paola introduces the 10 most common clouds and the weather they bring.

Try This! Over several days, have children sketch clouds for 5 minutes each day on an index card and record the date. Finally, have children sort their sketches and determine which cloud type they saw most and least often.

Is It a Shield for a Magnet?

Material	Prediction	Actual Result

ASKING QUESTIONS

(W) Whole-group activity   (S) Small-group activity

(I) Individual activity   (T) Transition   (RA) Read-aloud

(W) What Is Camouflage?

Before class, cut three fish each from orange construction paper, black construction paper, and newspaper. Invite children to sit in a large circle in the classroom. Ask them to close their eyes while you put a newspaper in the center of the group. Tell children to open their eyes and look at the newspaper. Next, have them close their eyes again as you place all nine fish on the newspaper. Tell children to open their eyes and quickly call out the number of fish they see. (Most children will see only the orange and black fish.) Discuss the word *camouflage* and how it protects many animals from their enemies.

To further expand children's knowledge about camouflage, read *What Color Is Camouflage?* by Carolyn Otto (HarperTrophy, 1996).

(W) Toothpick Toss

Buy a box of red toothpicks and a box of green toothpicks. Take children to a grassy area and have them stand in a large circle. Ask them to close their eyes, then toss 25 red and 25 green toothpicks in the center of the circle. When children open their eyes, ask what they see in the grass. Again, most children will see only the red toothpicks. (Make sure you count the toothpicks before tossing them in the grass, so you will know when all have been picked up after the experiment.)

W I Wonder...?

Model asking open-ended questions that require children to think and to use more than one word to answer the question:

- Why do you think that happened?
- What do you think might happen if...?
- How could we find out about...?

I How Do You Know?

When a child makes a statement about a science-related topic, stop for a moment and encourage the child to discuss the topic beyond the statement:

- How do you know that?
- Tell me why you think that.
- Have you ever seen something like that before?

Teaching Tip
Show how much you value a child's question by writing the question on an index card and asking the child to post it on an Inquiry Board in the science center. If you don't have time to answer the question or look for the answer, be sure to return to the question later.

S Find-the-Answer Center

For any science topic being studied by the class, gather books, pamphlets, magazine articles, encyclopedia articles, and Web sites related to that topic and keep them in a "find-the-answer" center. This will help children realize that answers to their questions can be found from many different resources. Model this activity for children by writing down their questions and using these resources to look up answers to those questions.

I Ask an Expert

Locate an expert in a science-related field who is willing to answer e-mailed questions. The expert could be a museum biologist, a parent of a child at your school who works as a geologist or botanist, or even a fourth-grade student who has had a pet guinea pig for three years. To establish some shared knowledge about the topic, choose one book to share with the class as a read-aloud. Then set up a center with the book, index cards, and pencils or markers. Children who choose this center can write questions to the expert. Have them read their question to a friend or two to make sure the question is easily understood, then invite them to type the question and e-mail it. Excitement and interest will build as the class receives answers. These answers will generate more questions.

W How Are Butterflies Different From Moths?

Use an insect net to capture a butterfly and a moth, or order butterflies and moths from a science catalog. Put butterflies in one jar and cover the jar's mouth with a nylon stocking held in place by a rubber band. Put moths in a separate jar. Place both jars and magnifying glasses in a learning center and encourage children to observe both insects a few minutes each day, from Monday to Thursday. On Friday, invite children to share the differences they observed between the insects.

To learn more about the differences between butterflies and moths, read *Amazing Butterflies and Moths* by John Still (Knopf, 1991). Place the book in the learning center so children can compare the photographs to the live specimens.

W Can We Make a Cricket Chirp More?

Pose this question to children and take a yes/no vote. Then tell them that you know how to make a cricket chirp more. Put a cricket in a glass jar and stretch a nylon stocking over the jar's mouth. Use a rubber band to hold the stocking in place. First thing in the morning, put the cricket outdoors in the shade. In 20 minutes, take children outside. Set a stopwatch for one minute, then ask children to count the number of cricket chirps in that minute. Repeat. Take the cricket back to the classroom and record both counts. Later in the day, repeat the activity and compare the different counts. (Note: Temperature affects many animals. In cool temperatures, crickets are somewhat sluggish; they are more active in warmer temperatures. The second counts should be higher because crickets chirp more during the warmest part of the day.)

Read *Chirping Crickets* by Melvin Berger (HarperTrophy, 1998) to gain more knowledge about crickets.

W All About Ants

Order an ant farm with live ants and set it up in the classroom to encourage questions about this insect. Place index cards and pencils near the ant farm so children can record their questions.

Read parts of *Very First Things to Know About Ants* by Patricia Grossman (Workman Publishing, 1997) over several days to find answers to children's questions.

W All About Mealworms

Create an environment for live mealworms, which can be purchased at most pet stores, by putting oatmeal in a glass jar. Set up the jar in the classroom to encourage questions about mealworms. Place index cards and pencils near the mealworms so children can record their questions.

Read parts of *Mealworms: Raise Them, Watch Them, See Them Change* by Adrienne Mason (Kids Can Press, 2001) over several days to find answers to children's questions.

W Student-Made Question-and-Answer Cards

Introduce children to BrainQuest®, a question-and-answer game for kids that can be found in many bookstores. Questions are organized around general themes, such as plants, animals, space, and so on. After playing this game a few times, distribute index cards to the class. Encourage children to create their own question-and-answer cards focused on a science topic studied recently. Punch a hole in one corner of the cards, then keep them together with a ring. Play the game during circle time or put the cards in the science center for small groups of children to play.

W Give Them the Words

Capitalize on teachable moments in your class. When a child notices a spiderweb in the corner of the classroom, take advantage of the moment to introduce vocabulary such as *arachnid, spinners, web,* and *orbs.* When two children discover an earthworm in the playground's flowerbed, use this opportunity to introduce the interdependence of plants and animals by explaining that earthworms enrich the soil.

Teaching Tip
For a new science topic, start a word wall of new vocabulary words near the science center.

I Who Lived Here?

Display a bird's nest in a plastic box. Have index cards and markers available. Challenge individual children to write questions about the nest, such as *"Which bird made it?" "What materials are in the nest?" "Where did the bird find the materials?"* and so on. After everyone has the opportunity to write questions, conduct an answer session.

Teaching Tip
Invite a local bird watcher to answer the class's
questions from the "Who Lived Here?" activity.

RA *The Grouchy Ladybug*
by Eric Carle (Thomas Crowell, 1977)

A grouchy ladybug refuses to share the aphids she sees on leaves. Instead, she spends her day challenging increasingly larger animals, who each have their own way of defending themselves.

Try This! Go through the book with children, and list all the animals the grouchy ladybug asks to fight.

Try This, Too! Assign an animal to a pair or small group of children. Ask them to draw the animal and answer the question, *"How does a _____ defend itself?"* On another day, have children choose an animal and write about how it defends itself. Use the book as reference as well as other books about each animal. If possible, pair a younger child with an older student from another class who reads well.

Try This, Too! If time allows, have small groups (and older partners) research how large each animal is, and make a reproduction of it. Children could mark off the length of each animal in school hallways.

RA *Did Dinosaurs Live in Your Backyard?: Questions and Answers About Dinosaurs*
by Melvin Berger (Scholastic, 1999)

This book contains questions and brief answers about a science topic that captures the attention of many young children—dinosaurs.

Try This! After studying a science-related topic, read Berger's book as a model for your own class book about the topic just completed. Invite the class to brainstorm enough questions so that each child has one question to answer. Have children write the answer to the question they get and draw a picture illustrating the facts. Bind the pages between cover stock and use Berger's title as a model for titling the book.

PREDICTING

W Whole-group activity **S** Small-group activity

I Individual activity **T** Transition **RA** Read-aloud

W How Hot Is It?

Ask children to predict which spot on the playground is the warmest and which one is the coolest. When no one else is on the playground, take children outside to test their predictions. Borrow enough thermometers so that every child can have two. Have children place their thermometers in the spots they predicted and wait five minutes before recording the temperatures. Return to the classroom and discuss what information they used to make their predictions and see how accurate their predictions were.

W Sink or Float?

Provide two or three containers of water. Ask children to look around the classroom and find three objects that will not be damaged if they get wet. Tell them that one object should be something they think will float, the second should be one they think will sink, and the third should be one that they're not sure of. Later, let children test their predictions by putting the objects in the water containers, then discuss results.

Reinforce children's experiments by reading *Sink and Float* by Deirdre Englehard (Instructional Fair, 1999).

RA *Who Sank the Boat?*
by Pamela Allen (Paper Star, 1996)

Several animals decide to row a boat in the bay. One by one the animals board the boat, but it sinks before they begin their adventure. Throughout the story, the reader considers the question raised at the beginning of the book: Who sank the boat?

W Vanishing Water

Provide three containers with very different surface areas, such as a small, shallow baking tin, a coffee cup, and a tall, slender cylinder. Pour one cup of water in each container, then put the containers on the same table in a low traffic part of the classroom. Ask children to predict if the water will evaporate from each container at the same time, or if one will evaporate first (and if so, which one). Record children's answers and observe the containers every day until all of the water evaporates from one or more containers. (Note: The water in the container with the largest surface area will evaporate first. That's because more water is exposed to the air, and so it evaporates faster.)

S What's in the Ice?

Divide the class into groups of six children. Give each group an ice-cube tray, a pitcher of water, and a flat pan. Ask each child to find two objects in the classroom that are small enough to fit into a section of the ice-cube tray. Have children place their items in the tray. As children pour water into the tray, ask them to predict what will happen when you put the ice-cube trays in a freezer.

Remove the trays from the freezer after two hours. Ask children if they can see both of their objects. Then dump the cubes onto the pan and ask children to find their two cubes. If a cube is too cloudy to see the object, hold it up to the light. Let the ice cubes melt, then ask children to predict whether the items will look the same as before they were frozen. Discuss whether the melted ice looks like the water poured from the pitcher.

S Heat Causes Changes

Have children observe and compare cookie dough, cheese, and ice before they are heated. Discuss the fact that heat causes change. Ask children to predict what will happen to each item when it is heated and record their predictions. Put each item in a toaster oven one at a time and observe the changes caused by the heat.

Ⓘ Will It Dissolve or Not?

Give each group of four children a muffin tin, four to six small bowls with assorted dry materials (for example, salt, cornstarch, flour, cornmeal, instant coffee, bouillon crystals), and stirrer sticks. Ask children to predict which materials will dissolve in water and which will not. Have them experiment to test their predictions.

Ⓢ Missing Pieces

Give each group of four to six children a simple machine, such as a small food grinder or small pencil sharpener. Have each child manipulate the machine, then predict what would happen if one component is removed. Have groups experiment to determine if the machine will work with less than the required parts.

Ⓢ Sun's Heat Makes a Treat

Give groups of six children a six-sectioned muffin tin, foil baking cups, six squares of a chocolate candy bar, and six marshmallows. Ask children to put each marshmallow in a baking cup and place the chocolate on top of the marshmallow. Ask them to predict what will happen after three minutes, six minutes, and nine minutes if the tin is placed under the hot sun. Take the tins outdoors and have children record their actual observations at three-minute intervals, comparing their predictions to actual outcomes.

Ⓢ Feely Bags

Gather enough pillowcases and familiar classroom or household objects so that each pair of children can have one. Hide an object in each pillowcase, then distribute a pillowcase to each pair. Ask children to identify the object using only their sense of touch.

① Rescuing Paper Clips

Give each student a steel paper clip and a glass filled with water. Ask children to suggest ways to get the paper clip out of the water. After a couple of minutes of brainstorming, ask children to predict how they could get the paper clip out of the water WITHOUT putting anything into the water, spilling any water, or getting their hands wet. Extend the discussion to include using a magnet, then provide each child with a magnet. Have children experiment until they discover the solution. (Note: If you hold the glass in one hand and the magnet in the other, you can put the magnet under the glass and move the paper clip to the side of the glass. Continue to move the magnet to the top of the glass where the paper clip will "jump" onto the magnet.)

① Sunlight Changes Color

Have children cut a 6-inch circle from card stock or a file folder. Have them place this circle on a 6-inch-square piece of red construction paper, using tape to attach the papers together. Place the papers near a window under direct sunlight. After two sunny days, remove the stiff paper and observe the change on the red construction paper. (Note: A light red or pink circle will be in the center of the red construction paper because energy from the sun causes some pigments to fade.)

① Growing Grass

Provide each student with a plastic cup, a tongue depressor, and two different-colored markers. Put containers of soil and grass seed on the table. Have children plant grass seed in their cups, then push the tongue depressor in the soil. Ask each child to predict how tall the grass will grow by the fifth day. Have them use one color to mark their prediction on the tongue depressor. Then have them predict how tall the grass will be on the tenth day and mark their prediction using the other color. After the tenth day, discuss the results with children. Then repeat the activity and check children's predictions to see if they are using what they learned.

1 Strongest of Three

Set up a center with three sizes of magnets, a small box of paper clips, masking tape, and copies of "How Strong Are Magnets?" (page 34). Have children tape one magnet to a table so that the magnet hangs over the edge of the table a bit.

Unbend one end of a paper clip and stick it to the magnet. Hang other paper clips on the open end until the group of paper clips falls to the ground. Count the paper clips and record the number on the recording sheet. Repeat the activity. Next, tape the second magnet on the table and repeat the activity. Repeat again with the third magnet. When every child has had an opportunity to complete these activities, ask all children to bring their recording sheets to a group meeting and discuss whether or not they think the size or shape of a magnet affects its strength.

To learn more about magnets, read *What Makes a Magnet?* by Franklyn M. Branley (HarperTrophy, 1996).

1 Mystery Reaction

Give every child a small, clear plastic cup and an eyedropper. Give each group of four children a container of finely ground black pepper and a small container of liquid soap. Help children fill their cup half full of water. Ask them to sprinkle pepper on the water's surface and observe what the pepper does. Then have children predict what will happen when a drop of soap is added to the middle of the water. Invite children to drop the soap, watch what happens, and compare the results to their predictions.

1 Seeds

Place a variety of seeds, a divided tray for sorting, magnifying glasses, and pencils and paper on a table. On a wall near the table, post a picture of the fully grown plant for each type of seed. Ask children to predict which seed would produce which fruit or vegetable. For the most effective activity, ensure that there are very small seeds (for example, tomato and radish), larger seeds (corn, beans), and very large seeds (avocado, peaches).

Ⅰ Sprouting Eyes

Bring in several potatoes that have begun to sprout. Explain to children that you do not always need seeds to grow a new plant. Ask each child to use a plastic knife to cut a piece of potato, making sure that an eye is on the piece. Provide each student with a paper cup with a small hole punched through its bottom, potting soil, and a plate. Have each child plant their potato piece one inch deep in the soil, water the soil, then place the cup and plate in a sunny place. Have each child predict how long it will take to see the first sprout and record the predictions. Over the next several days, remind children to keep the soil moist and observe the soil very carefully so that they can see the first bit of green.

Ⅰ Bottle Blow Out

Collect a small, empty plastic soda bottle for each child. Distribute one bottle and one balloon to each child. Have children push the deflated balloon into the bottle and stretch the open end of the balloon over the bottle's mouth. Ask children to predict what will happen to the balloon when they blow air into it, and write their predictions. Then challenge each child to blow up his or her balloon and try to explain what actually happens. (Note: The balloon will do nothing. Air takes up space, so the bottle is already full of air. When a child tries to blow up the balloon, the air trapped inside the bottle presses against the balloon, preventing it from inflating.)

RA *This Year's Garden*
by Cynthia Rylant (Aladdin, 1987)

Children will enjoy this lovely explanation of the cycle of a garden.

Try This! Have children predict how many seeds are in fruits that they eat for lunch. Then have the owner of the fruit count the seeds and report back to the class after lunch.

Try This, Too! Plant several varieties of seeds and care for them in the class-room until they become large enough to transplant in an outdoor garden.

Name _____ **Date** _____

How Strong Are Magnets?

Magnet One

Kind of Magnet	First Try	Second Try
	(How many paper clips can it hold?)	(How many paper clips can it hold?)

Magnet Two

Kind of Magnet	First Try	Second Try
	(How many paper clips can it hold?)	(How many paper clips can it hold?)

Magnet Three

Kind of Magnet	First Try	Second Try
	(How many paper clips can it hold?)	(How many paper clips can it hold?)

EXPERIMENTING

W Whole-group activity   **S** Small-group activity

I Individual activity   **T** Transition   **RA** Read-aloud

I Oil and Water Just Don't Mix

Tape a place mat–sized piece of waxed paper on a flat surface for each child. Have children use an eyedropper to put 10 drops of water and 10 drops of oil on the waxed paper. Suggest that they drop water on top of oil and oil on top of water. Have children blow on their drops using a straw and see what happens. Discuss the results of their experiments and answer the question: Can oil and water mix?

I More Mixing Methods

Give each child a clear plastic cup, an eyedropper, and oil. Have children fill their cups half full of water, then use the eyedropper to add oil to the water. Ask them to observe what happens very closely. Challenge them to get the water and oil to mix.

W Hot Fabric

Using a desk lamp as a heat source, put three pieces of fabric—a white one, a black one, and a shiny metallic one—under the lamp. Wait five minutes, turn off the lamp, and immediately place strip thermometers on each cloth. Have children hypothesize the reasons for the difference in temperatures (white and metallic cloths reflect heat, while black cloth absorbs it).

W Hot Water

Fill two quart jars with cool water from the same water source. Tape a piece of white construction paper around one jar, and a piece of black construction paper around the other. Record the temperature in both jars, then set them out in the sun on top of white paper. Over the next three hours, ask student volunteers to record the hourly temperature for both jars. Compare temperatures and discuss.

S "Leaking" Water Bottles

Divide the class into small groups of four to six children. Provide each group with two widemouthed, clear plastic bottles with lids, crushed ice, cold water, warm tap water, food coloring, and paper towels.

Have children fill one bottle with ice and cold water, and the second bottle with warm water. Put several drops of food coloring into each bottle, put on their lids, then place both bottles on a paper towel. Ask children to use as many of their senses as they can to make observations. Ask them to describe similarities and differences between the bottles. If necessary, guide children to observe that the condensation on the cold-water bottle is not colored, and therefore could not have leaked through the bottle. Explain condensation.

S Weighty Issues

Fill three same-size containers with three similar-looking substances (for example, white sand, salt, and cream of wheat). Ask children to predict which container is the lightest and which is the heaviest. Then have them use a balance scale to explore the relative weight of the three containers.

To extend this activity, repeat the experiment using three larger containers and three smaller containers. Remind children that scientists often repeat experiments many times to ensure that their results are accurate.

S Creating Crystals

Divide the class into groups of three children. Provide each group with black construction paper, scissors, a pie pan (or shallow bowl), warm water, Epsom salt, a tablespoon, and a measuring cup.

First, have children cut the black paper so that it fits in the bottom of the pie pan. Have each group add 1 tablespoon of Epsom salt to 1/4 cup of warm water and stir until the salt dissolves. Next, pour the salty water onto the black paper in the pie pan. Put all the pie pans in the sun and check them over several days until all of the water evaporates. Then invite children to observe the newly formed crystals.

S Mini Volcanoes

Place a glass bottle with a narrow neck in the middle of a round pan. Build a mountain of clay around the bottle to hold it steady. Use a funnel to pour approximately 1/4 cup of baking soda into the bottle. Then add a teaspoon of liquid dish detergent, and pour 1/4 cup of vinegar into the bottle (color the vinegar red for effect). Watch as the mini volcano erupts.

To learn more about real volcanoes, read *Volcanoes* by Franklyn Branley (HarperTrophy, 1986).

S Funnel Play

Fill a large plastic container half full of water. Provide several sizes of funnels, clear plastic bottles, and cups for pouring water. Encourage children to experiment with the materials, predicting and testing their predictions about how water goes through different sizes of funnels.

S Create Sandstone

Provide a small group with four cups of clean sand, two cups of water, two cups of cornstarch, and an old pan. Have children stir the ingredients until well mixed, then (with an adult volunteer supervising) put the pan on a hot plate and heat until the mixture is thick. After the mixture cools, divide it among the children and encourage them to sculpt a figure.

Show photographs of natural sandstone formations to help children make connections between their sculptures and how nature sculpts sandstone with wind and water.

S Bubble Shapes

Provide each group of four children with the following materials: florist wire cut into 18-inch lengths, a dishpan, one cup of Joy® dishwashing liquid, and access to water and measuring cups.

First, have children make different-shaped bubble wands from the florist wire. Suggest making squares, ovals, triangles, rectangles—anything but circles. Tell children to make a bubble solution by pouring the liquid soap into the dishpan, adding eight cups of water, and stirring the solution. Have children experiment by making bubbles with different wands and observing the shape of the bubble that comes out of each shaped wand. (Note: All bubbles will be round because there is no greater force on any part of the bubble to give it a shape other than a circle.)

To gain more knowledge about bubbles, read *Pop: A Book About Bubbles* by Kimberly Brubaker Bradley (HarperCollins, 2001).

S What Makes the Best Bubbles?

After children have made their own bubble mixture in the "Bubble Shapes" experiment above, pose this question: What makes the best bubbles? Provide children with various kinds of liquid, flaked, and bar soaps, and challenge children to create the best bubbles they can.

Read *I Wonder Why Soap Makes Bubbles* by Barbara Taylor (Kingfisher, 1994) for more information about bubbles.

S Racing Drops of Water

Cover a cookie sheet with wax paper, then put one end of the cookie sheet on a block to make an inclined plane. Ask each child in the group to mix water with a few drops of food coloring. Invite children to experiment with dropping one drop at a time in the same place. Ask them to note how many drops it takes to make the water roll down the cookie sheet.

On another day, repeat the activity with water that has several drops of liquid soap added to it. On another day, change the angle of the cookie sheet. Each time, note how many drops it takes to make the water droplet begin to move.

S The Nose Knows

In a center, place peeled apple pieces and peeled raw potatoes, a grater, two identical bowls, a marker, and stick-on labels. Label the bottom of one bowl *Apple* and the other *Potato*. Have children work in pairs or small groups to grate the apple and potato into the appropriate bowls. Taking turns, each child should hold his or her nose and taste each food. Then the same child should taste each food without holding his or her nose. Have children discuss which way made it easier to distinguish between the two foods and why they think that is. (Note: The senses of smell and taste work together. The odor of food helps people distinguish subtle flavors.)

To expand children's knowledge about their sense of smell, read *Smell: The Library of the Five Senses and the Sixth Sense* by Sue Hurwitz (Franklin Watts, 1999).

I How Do My Bean Plants Grow?

Provide each child with two sandwich-size resealable plastic bags, two paper towels, and four lima beans. Label the bags with each child's name. Show children how to wet the paper towel, fold it to keep the beans inside, then carefully put the paper towel inside the plastic bag. Have each child tape one bag on a window and one in the dark. Over several days observe what happens. Have children make an entry in their journals every other day, recording their observations of the bean plants' growth.

(S) Testing Growing Conditions

Divide the class into two groups. Repeat the "How Do My Bean Plants Grow?" experiment with the first group taping one bag in a cool place and another one in a warm place. Have the second group tape both bags where they will get sunlight, but keep one damp and the other dry. Have children predict what will happen to each of their lima beans and observe to test their predictions.

(I) One Color or Two?

Provide a glass, white paper towels cut into 1-inch-wide strips, and a water-based green marker (not permanent). Have children color a stripe of green two inches from one end of a paper strip. Then have them pour an inch of water into the glass, and predict what will happen when the strip is placed in the water. Set the strip in the glass so that the green stripe is one inch above the water. Invite children to observe the water as it moves up the strip of paper. (Note: The green ink will separate into blue and yellow.)

On other days, repeat the experiment using different colored markers. Each day, ask children to predict what will happen to the color selected before doing the experiment. Keep a record of what happens with each color. After several days, explain the difference between primary and secondary colors.

(I) Is It Solid or Liquid?

Give each child the following materials: 1 cup of cornstarch, 1/2 cup of water, a bowl, a spoon, and a small bottle of food coloring (optional).

Have children put the cornstarch into the bowl, then slowly add water, constantly stirring. When the mixture reaches the consistency of thick pancake batter, stop adding water. (Warn children NOT to add in all of the water at once; they may not need the entire half cup of water.) Add a few drops of food coloring and stir. Finally, invite children to feel the mixture with their hands, roll some of it into a ball, and put the ball on a table. Later in the day, distribute copies of "My Experiment Report" (page 44), and ask children to complete it.

❶ Dancing Popcorn

Ask children to put several pieces of unpopped popcorn kernels in a glass of water. Add a teaspoon of vinegar and a teaspoon of baking soda and watch what happens. (Note: Bubbles created by the vinegar and baking soda mixture will carry the kernels up and down the glass of water.)

❶ Rollin' Down the Incline

Construct a simple incline using cardboard propped up at a 30-degree angle. Provide several objects—small balls, paper-towel tubes, thread spools, 1-inch cubes, linking cubes—for children to experiment with. Some objects will roll easily down the incline and some will not. When every student in the class has had the opportunity to experiment with the objects, lead a discussion about the differences between the object that rolled the fastest (or the farthest) and the objects that would not roll at all.

❶ Racing Down the Incline

Make a second incline exactly the same as in the above activity, but cover it with sandpaper. Provide several small cars for children to roll down the inclines. Lead a discussion about the differences in the two ramps and the sandpaper's effect on the speed of the cars.

Then, remove the sandpaper and replace it with a different material such as fabric, waxed paper, or aluminum foil. Have children predict which material will make the cars go faster (or slower) than on the plain incline.

❶ When Milk Meets Soap

Give each child a small, shallow container (a petri dish works well). Fill each container half full of whole milk. Tell children to put two drops of food coloring in the four quadrants of the container (draw a sketch so children understand the term *quadrant*). Ask them to predict what will happen when they add a couple of drops of liquid soap in the middle of the container. (Note: The soap interacts with the fat in the milk and causes the food coloring to swirl.)

Teaching Tip
Have children conduct the "When Milk Meets Soap" experiment on top of several sheets of paper towels, just in case spills occur.

Ⓘ Creating High, Creating Low

Give each child four plastic cups and 20 rubber bands of different sizes. Ask them to experiment with different combinations of rubber bands wrapped around the cups to create one cup that makes a high sound and another cup that makes a low sound.

On the following day, repeat the experiment, replacing the plastic cups with plastic margarine containers. The next day replace the plastic items with wooden blocks. Each day the children's goal is to create one object that makes a high sound and one that makes a low sound.

Ⓘ A Musical Experiment

Following a group discussion about how children created high and low sounds in the above experiment, set up a center with all of the materials used in the experiment, plus small boxes, cardboard, tape, and string. Challenge children to create a musical instrument that makes both high and low sounds.

Ⓢ Rock Throwing

Have children collect six rocks: two small ones, two large ones, and two in-between ones. Ask each child to predict which rock will travel farthest when thrown, which one will be the easiest to throw, and which one will be the hardest to throw. With adult supervision, let three children at a time go outside on the playground (when no one else is outside) and toss their six rocks. Have each student record the results. The next day, conduct a class discussion about what they found out. Compare findings to see if most children got the same results.

1 Finding Meteorites

To make a "meteorite finder," distribute a paper cup, a pencil, string, and a magnet to each child. Help children use the pencil to poke three holes into the cup just below the rim. Then show each child how to thread string through each hole, leaving the string long enough to reach from a child's hand to the floor. Tie knots to hold the strings in the cup, then pull the strings above the cup and tie. Place a strong magnet in the cup.

Later in the day, take the meteorite finder outside and walk on the side-walk holding the meteorite finder just above the ground. Listen for small clinks. Pieces of rock the magnet attracts might just be meteorites, because these "rocks" contain iron and nickel.

RA *What Is the World Made Of?*
All About Solids, Liquids, and Gases
by Kathleen Weidner Zoehfeld (Scott Foresman, 1998)

The author explains the difficult concepts of solid, liquid, and gas in simple, informal text.

Try This! Have children observe the process of the solid ice melting into liquid water (use a hair dryer to speed the process). Later, watch the water turn into gas water vapor when boiled.

Try This, Too! Alternatively, place a few ice cubes (solid) in an electric skillet. Turn on the heat and let children watch as the ice melts (liquid). Continue to heat the water until it boils. Then hold a cookie sheet over the skillet to catch the water vapor (gas), and turn it into water again. Be sure children stay safely away from the cord and skillet.

RA *Levers*
by Sally M. Walker and Roseann Feldmann (Lerner, 2001)

This book explains levers, from seesaws to light switches and wheelbarrows. It also offers instructions for exploring with levers.

Name _____ **Date** _____

My Experiment Report

What I did: _____

_____

_____

_____

What I observed: _____

_____

_____

_____

MEASURING AND ESTIMATING

Ⓦ Whole-group activity   Ⓢ Small-group activity

Ⓘ Individual activity   Ⓣ Transition   ⓇⒶ Read-aloud

Ⓦ How Many Shoes Long Am I?

Bring several pairs of your shoes to school and line them against a wall, heel to toe. Ask a volunteer to lie down beside the shoes then count how many shoes long the child is. Record the shoe measurements and graph the results if time permits. Repeat this activity on another day using shoes from children in the class.

ⓇⒶ *How Big Is a Foot?*
by Rolf Myller (Scott Foresman, 1991)

In this story, the King's carpenter tries to measure and make a bed for the Queen's birthday. The lowly carpenter measures with his foot while the King measures with his larger foot. The concept of "ruler" meaning "one foot" can be handily explained with this book.

S Inchworm Measurement

Organize children into pairs, giving each pair a copy of the "Big Hand" (page 49). Have children cut out the inchworms and lay them on top of the Big Hand to measure it. Ask the pairs to predict whether their hands are larger or smaller than the Big Hand, then measure using the inchworms to test their predictions.

S How Much Water?

Gather plastic tools used for measuring liquids (measuring cups, measuring spoons) and place them in a learning center with a large tub of water. Encourage children to explore the relationship between the different containers; for example, how many teaspoons of water fill up 1/4 cup?

S How Long Is It?

Gather tools used for measuring length (6-inch rulers, 12-inch rulers, measuring tapes, yardsticks) and place them in a learning center. Encourage children to use these tools to measure objects in the classroom. Include some manipulatives, such as paper clips, blocks, and links, for nonstandard measurement as well.

S Measuring a Snack

Set up a snack center where children can create their own drinks. Vary the ingredients for the drinks depending on children's preferences and the cost of different items. (Make sure to check for food allergies first.) The important part of this activity is that children practice using measuring cups and measuring spoons. Here's one recipe that meets this requirement:

> 1/2 cup of orange juice
>
> 2/3 cup of pineapple juice
>
> 1 cup of lemon-lime soda
>
> 1 tablespoon of juice from a bottle of maraschino cherries

S Colder Than Ice

Have children work in pairs to fill a container with one cup of water. Put a thermometer in the water and record its temperature. Ask them to fill an identical container with ice, cover the ice with water, and record its temperature. Have children carefully stir one tablespoon of salt into the ice water and record the temperature again. Add another tablespoon of salt, stir, and record the temperature one last time. Have children compare the recorded temperatures and discuss. (Note: Salt requires energy to dissolve. This energy comes from heat in the water, so the water gets colder as the salt uses the water's heat.)

I Measuring Tools

Ask each child to bring from home different devices used to measure something (make sure their names are on each tool). Divide these tools into groups—those that measure length, weight, volume, temperature, and so on—and discuss each. Examples include rulers, yardsticks, measuring tape, retractable tape, balance scales, bathroom scales, measuring cups, measuring spoons, and thermometers.

I Measuring the Rain

Provide children with a two-liter soda bottle (cut off the top of the bottle so eight inches remain), one cup of gravel, a ruler, clear tape, and tap water. Help children place the pebbles in the bottom of the soda bottle, then tape the ruler to the side of the bottle with the zero end touching the pebbles. Fill the bottle with water until it reaches the zero end of the ruler. To measure the amount of rain that falls, place the rain gauge outdoors during a rain shower. If there is no rain in the forecast, children could take the rain gauges home to measure the water flow of their shower in one minute.

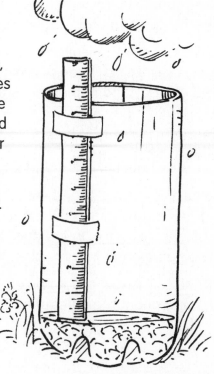

(RA) *Measuring Penny*
by Loreen Leedy (Henry Holt, 1998)

Leedy introduces various kinds of measurement (height, weight, volume, even time and temperature) and units of measurement. For a homework assignment, Lisa measures her dog, Penny, with all kinds of nonstandard measurement, and finds ways to measure all kinds of things about Penny.

Try This! This book provides excellent opportunities for children to mimic the activities of the main character. Following the read-aloud, make a list of all the ways Lisa measured her dog and decide how many of those ways could be used to measure a person. Then have children complete this activity as a homework assignment, just like Lisa did.

Try This, Too! The use of nonstandard measurement in this book can lead to using many different types of nonstandard measurement—how tall is each child in paper clips, interlocking cubes, rectangular unit blocks, markers, and so on.

(RA) *Albert's Alphabet*
by Leslie Tryon (Aladdin, 1994)

The school principal asks Albert the Goose to build an alphabet for the playground. He has no time to go to the store to buy supplies, so he uses what he can find around the school.

Try This! Challenge children to identify the different measuring tools that Albert uses. List children's answers on chart paper, or ask children to draw the tools they find in the pages of the book.

(RA) *Titch*
by Pat Hutchins (Aladdin, 1993)

Titch is the youngest and smallest of three children. He always gets the smallest of any item—the smallest bike, the smallest kite, the smallest musical instrument. In the end, Titch's smallest seeds grow larger than anything belonging to his older brother and sister.

Try This! This is a great book for introducing sorting objects into small, medium, and large categories.

Big Hand

Inchworms

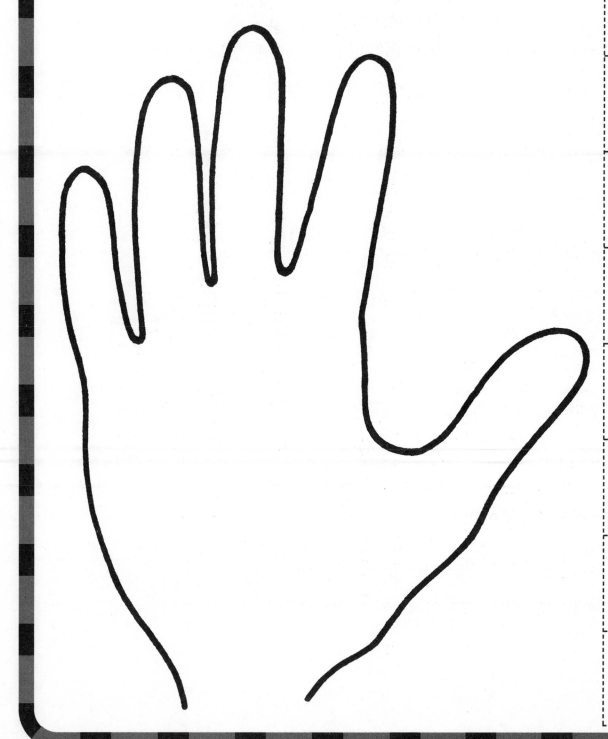

DESIGNING AND MAKING MODELS

W Whole-group activity   **S** Small-group activity

I Individual activity   **T** Transition   **RA** Read-aloud

S Balloon Races

Provide one helium balloon for each group of four children. Have children work together to attach a small paper cup to the string on their balloon, then put sufficient weight (buttons, coins, or paper clips) into the cup to suspend the balloon in midair. Establish a starting line and a finish line, then have a balloon race. Repeat the race with a box fan, or race the balloons outside. Discuss the difference in how the balloons responded in each race.

I Rolling Marbles

Put a construction set of Marbleworks® in a center by itself. Challenge individual children to create a structure through which a marble can roll among connected parts. Photograph and post each child's construction. Challenge children to complete the structure in less than 10 minutes.

S Straw Alphabet

Read *Albert's Alphabet* by Leslie Tryon (Aladdin, 1994), a book about a goose who builds an alphabet for a school playground. Then provide plastic straws,

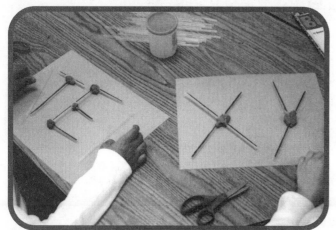

scissors, tape, and modeling clay for each small group. Encourage children to use these materials to construct one letter as Albert did. Challenge children to return to these materials during their self-selected activity time to make as many letters of the alphabet as they can.

Teaching Tip
As groups of children create the letters of the alphabet, they will quickly run out of room at their tables. Have aluminum foil (or other material) available so they can make an out-of-the-way place to put their letters.

I Marshmallow Bridges

Set up a center so that individual children can explore building with different sizes of marshmallows and toothpicks. After a few days of exploration, challenge children to work alone or in pairs to build a bridge between two chairs. Suggest that children try different construction strategies to determine what makes the strongest and most stable bridge.

S Marshmallow Book Support

For each group of three children, provide 15 marshmallows and 20 toothpicks. Challenge them to use what they learned in the "Marshmallow Bridges" activity above to make a structure strong enough to hold a book. Have children test their structures. If children are struggling, ask them whether they need to think about surface area, or if they need to use more triangles in the structure.

Teaching Tip
Children will be less likely to eat manipulatives such as
marshmallows if they know in advance that they will be allowed
to eat them when the activity is completed.

S Strong Paper

Invite children to explore folding paper into
"strong shapes," such as cylinders, triangles,
squares, and zigzags. Have them stand the
folded paper on end and determine which
shape supports the most weight. Use pieces
of cardboard that have been precut into 6-inch
squares as the weight to test. Have children
stack pieces of cardboard on the folded paper
very carefully to see how many each shape
can support.

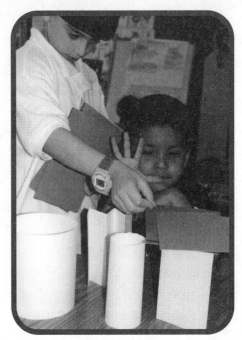

I Float the Boat

Ask children to form modeling clay
into the shape of a boat. Provide a
few small tubs of water so children
can try to float their boats. Then ask
them to place pennies in the boat
one at a time very carefully. Have
each child display his or her boat
along with the number of pennies it held before sinking.

Extend this experiment by challenging children to make an aluminum-foil
boat that will hold a certain weight (for example, five pennies) without sinking.

① Saltwater Float

Save all the boats from the "Float the Boat" activity and repeat the experiment using salt water. Ask children to make predictions about what will happen with the clay and aluminum foil boats.

RA *Feel the Wind*
by Arthur Dorros (Scott Foresman, 1990)

Dorros explains about wind—what causes it, how it affects the weather, and how people use the wind for help—in words simple enough for young children to understand. At the end of the book, you'll find directions for building a simple weather vane.

Try This! Provide the necessary materials for small groups of children to build the weather vane Dorros describes in his book.

RA *Building a House*
by Byron Barton (William Morrow, 1981)

Using simple words and drawings, Barton leads the reader through the process of building a house.

Try This! Place the book in a center, opening it to the page featuring the house's frame. Stock the center with craft sticks and several adhesive materials (white glue, glue stick, masking tape, and Scotch tape) for attaching the sticks together. Challenge children to create a model for framing a house.

RA *Galimoto*
by Karen Lynn Williams (Mulberry, 1991)

Kondi, an African child, spends the entire day collecting wire so that he can make a *galimoto*. Half the fun of this story is trying to figure out what a *galimoto* is.

Try This! Enhance this read-aloud by giving children pipe cleaners and challenging them to create their own *galimotos*.

FINDING PATTERNS AND RELATIONSHIPS

W Whole-group activity   **S** Small-group activity

I Individual activity   **T** Transition   **RA** Read-aloud

S How Many Circles? How Many Squares?

Send children on a shapes hunt. For younger children, encourage pairs to look for shapes in the classroom—circles, rectangles, squares, triangles—then allow them to share what they identified. For older children, distribute clipboards, paper, and pencils. Ask them to record as many shapes as they can identify in two minutes. As each child reports to the class, record the answers, placing tally marks beside objects identified by more than one child.

W Day, Night, Day, Night: The Patterns in Our Lives

Divide the class into two groups. Ask one group to draw things that they do during the day, and the other group to draw things they do during the evening. Using their drawings, have children create patterns that alternate day and night activities.

S Day to Day: The Patterns on Our Calendar

Create patterns on a calendar. Begin by posting circles on even-numbered days and squares on odd-numbered days. Review the pattern with small groups, then ask children to extend the patterns to upcoming days with circles or squares. You can also use commercially available shape templates instead of circles and squares.

S Patterns, Patterns Everywhere

Divide the class into groups of four. Send each group with an adult volunteer (or an older student) to conduct a quick assessment of patterns in the school building.

S Playing Season to Season

Have children work in groups of three or four to create summer, spring, autumn, and winter patterns using photographs of children playing outdoors during each season.

Teaching Tip

Young children are drawn to photographs of themselves and their friends. Take photographs for the "Playing Season to Season" activity, beginning on the first week of school to represent summer, and during obvious fall, winter, and spring scenes. Then present the activity to children in the last few weeks of school. If this is not possible, children could identify photographs in magazines representing each season of the year.

S Arachnid Patterns

Go on a short walking field trip around the school and search for spiderwebs. If one is in reach, carefully approach the web with a piece of black poster-board. If you touch the spiderweb just right, it will adhere to the posterboard, making it easy to take back to the classroom for close observation.

To learn more about spiders and how they make their webs, read *Spider* by Gail Gibbons (Holiday House, 1994). In her explanation of spiders, Gibbons describes different variations of spiderwebs.

I One of a Kind

Set up a center with copies of the "Fingerprint Chart" (page 59), white paper, soft lead pencils, clear tape, and a magnifying glass. Post a copy of common fingerprint patterns. Have each child rub the pencil on a piece of paper to make a large black mark. Next, have children rub the end of their left little finger on the black pencil mark and attach a one-inch piece of tape to their fingertip. Remove the tape and place it on the "left hand" chart above "pinkie finger." Repeat the same process for each finger. Encourage children to examine their fingerprints to determine patterns.

I Leaf Similarity

Give each child a clipboard, a crayon, and several pieces of 6-inch square tissue paper, then go outside. Ask children to select a leaf, place it on the clipboard, and cover it with a piece of tissue paper. Ask them to gently rub a crayon over the paper to create a leaf rubbing. Children can make as many rubbings as they can in the time limit you set. Later have children work alone or in pairs to sort leaves by varying patterns.

To extend children's knowledge about leaves, read *Why Do Leaves Change Colors?* by Betsy Maestro (HarperTrophy, 1996). In her discussion of leaves, Maestro describes leaves in different sizes, shapes, and colors. She also includes simple instructions for making a leaf rubbing and for pressing leaves.

T Verbal Patterns

Chant patterns related to science concepts, such as day/night/day/night..., winter/spring/summer/fall/winter/spring/summer/fall..., egg/caterpillar/chrysalis/butterfly/egg/caterpillar/chrysalis/butterfly..., and so on.

① Ordering Music

Use a permanent marker to label five glass soda bottles at varying heights. Mark one bottle at 1 inch from the bottom, one at 1 1/2 inches, and the other bottles at 2 inches, 2 1/2 inches, and 3 inches from the bottom. Pour water to the line on each bottle. Then invite each child in turn to tap each bottle with spoon or pencil near the top and organize the bottles in order based on pitch. Have the child record the way he or she organized the bottles by drawing each bottle and its water level.

After everyone has had the opportunity to experiment with creating sounds, discuss the results with the class and ask children to predict why they turned out that way. (Note: The bottle with the least amount of water vibrates the most and has the highest pitch.) Encourage children to create musical patterns by tapping on the bottles.

ⓇⒶ *Lots and Lots of Zebra Stripes: Patterns in Nature*
by Steven Swinburne (Boyds Mills Press, 1998)

Swinburne opens this book with a definition of patterns: lines and shapes that repeat. The beautiful photographs show readers patterns in nature, including watermelons, pumpkins, spiderwebs, and snakes. The book also encourages children to look for all kinds of patterns in nature, such as in flowers and insects.

Try This! Take children on a quick nature walk or a stroll through the neigborhood. Encourage them to look for patterns and allow them to sketch or photograph the patterns they find.

RA *Nature's Paintbrush: The Patterns and Colors Around You*
by Susan Stockdale (Simon & Schuster, 1998)

Using the zoo in Atlanta and a local science center as inspiration, Stockdale shows the reader different patterns and colors in nature through her bold acrylic paintings. She opens each section with a question, such as *"Have you ever touched a starfish?"* Her answers are brief, simply worded explanations of how animals use patterns and colors to protect themselves from enemies, attract mates, and warn other animals that they are dangerous.

Try This! Encourage children to create paintings in the style of this artist/illustrator.

RA *Pattern*
by Henry Pluckrose (Children's Press, 1995)

Every page of this book is a full-page photograph with a statement or a question superimposed on the photo. Most of the photographs are science-related, including butterfly wings, peacock feathers, a drop of water in a pond, and so on.

Try This! Using the book as a model, encourage children to find patterns in and around the school. Let each child take a photograph. Later, invite children to dictate or write a sentence related to their photographs. Bind all the pages into a book called "Patterns in Our School."

Teaching Tip
Take your class's pattern photographs with a digital camera. Use a word processing program to write captions over the photos.

Name _____ Date _____

Fingerprint Chart

Loop

Whorl

Arch

This is my left hand:

Pinkie finger	Ring finger	Middle finger	Index finger	Thumb

This is my right hand:

Thumb	Index finger	Middle finger	Ring finger	Pinkie finger

COMMUNICATING

W Whole-group activity   **S** Small-group activity

I Individual activity   **T** Transition   **RA** Read-aloud

W Guess What I See?

Pose "guess-what-I-see" descriptions to the whole class using very detailed language. When possible, use language that describes more than one of the senses. This models for children the language they can use to put their observations into words. For example, when describing a daisy, say, "*I see something in the classroom that has three different colors. Part of it feels soft and part of it feels rough. It smells sweet. It makes absolutely no noise.*" You can play this game outdoors as well.

W K-W-L Knowledge Chart

Divide chart paper into three sections: *K*, *W*, and *L*. When beginning a new science topic, ask children what they already know about the topic. Record their answers on the *K* part of the chart: What We <u>K</u>now. The next day, ask children what they want to know about the topic. Record their answers on the *W* part: What We <u>W</u>ant to Know. Throughout the unit of study, spend a few minutes filling in the third part of the chart—What We've <u>L</u>earned—and adding to the *W* section as children present new questions. Creating this graphic organizer models for children how to organize information.

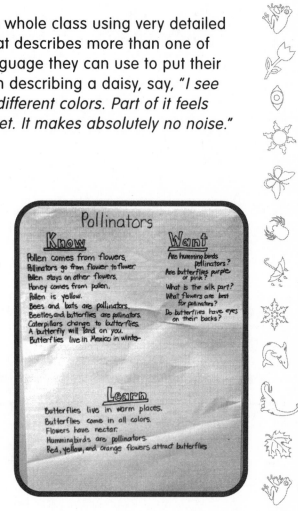

Pollinators

Know
Pollen comes from flowers.
Pollinators go from flower to flower.
Pollen stays on other flowers.
Honey comes from pollen.
Pollen is yellow.
Bees and bats are pollinators.
Beetles and butterflies are pollinators.
Caterpillars change to butterflies.
A butterfly will land on you.
Butterflies live in Mexico in winter.

Want
Are humming birds pollinators?
Are butterflies purple or pink?
What is the silk part?
What flowers are best for pollinators?
Do butterflies have eyes on their backs?

Learn
Butterflies live in warm places.
Butterflies come in all colors.
Flowers have nectar.
Hummingbirds are pollinators.
Red, yellow, and orange flowers attract butterflies

W Field Journals

Take children on a 10-minute nature walk on the playground with the goal of collecting science specimens, such as rocks, leaves, insects, and blades of grass. Before starting the field trip, talk to children about the entries that scientists make in their journals to record information about the specimens they collect (including date, place, observations and descriptions, and measurements).

W Collection Catalog

Ask children to catalog the specimens they collected in the "Field Journals" activity above. Have them assign a sequential number to each specimen as it is collected, and make sure the catalog number corresponds to the description in the collector's field journal.

W Picture File Chats

Introduce scientific language that relates to a group of pictures and encourage children to use that language to describe what they see in the pictures. For example, collect 10 to 12 large pictures of habitats—forest, mountain, desert, swamp, seashore, ocean, coral, rain forest, river, lake, scrubland, tundra, and savannah—and introduce vocabulary that relates to these habitats.

W What Animals Need

Bring a small mammal, such as a guinea pig or hamster, into the classroom and let children observe the animal for a few days. Over a five-day period, take a few minutes each day to discuss the animal's needs for food, water, air, proper environment, and waste removal. Emphasize vocabulary specific to that animal.

Read books about small mammals, such as *Guinea Pigs Don't Read Books* by Colleen Stanley Bare (Puffin, 1993), which explains what guinea pigs do and do not do. Photographs of different kinds of guinea pigs add clarity to the book.

W Charting Animal Needs

Create a chart listing the five important things that pets need—food, water, air, proper environment, and waste removal—across the top. Write the name of the small animal (from the previous activity) on the left side of the chart and record its information in that row. The next week repeat the same observations and conversations with a new animal, writing the name of

that animal on a new row and recording information about it in that row. This can be repeated for as many pets as you and your children can borrow for a week of observation in the classroom.

W Depending on Others

Compare the ways babies depend on their parents and the ways classroom pets depend on children. Create a comparison chart of how babies and pets depend on others for food, water, and a place to live and play.

(S) Discovery Table

Set up a discovery table in the classroom. Select intriguing items that are related to science, and change the item on the table each week. Children will be drawn to these items and begin to look forward to the new item each week.

Teaching Tip

Nature provides fascinating items for children to explore. Some of the objects to include on a discovery table are interesting seashells, fossils, a caged animal borrowed for a week, an unfamiliar fruit or vegetable, or an unusual plant such as a cactus or Venus flytrap. A specimen of coprolite invariably fascinates young children. These oddly shaped "rocks" can be purchased over the Internet. Coprolites are actually fossilized dinosaur poop!

(S) Soil From the U.S.A.

Help children write to people in different parts of the country, asking each person to send a soil sample in a film canister to the class. (Ask families for names and addresses of friends who would be willing to participate.) For example, you might collect red clay from Georgia, sandy soil from Florida, topsoil from Iowa, sand from west Texas, or soil from a Maine forest. Label each canister as it arrives, then put half of the soil into a labeled resealable bag. When you've gathered several, compare the soil samples.

I Illustrating Science

Explain to children that scientists often communicate their observations through sketches. Set up a science sketching learning center. For several weeks, place a new item in the center for children to observe very carefully and sketch in as much detail as they can. For example, children could sketch an iris one week. Another week, they could use magnifying glasses to study their thumbprints.

I How Do Rocks Smell?

Display rocks, soil, and water in separate containers. Ask children to observe, touch, hold, and smell each type of material, then describe how each one looks, feels, and smells.

T Be a Tree

Put on an environmental tape of wind and ask children to "plant their roots" and move to the wind—slowly for gentle breezes and quickly for strong winds.

RA *Water Dance*
by Thomas Locker (Harcourt, 1997)

"I am one thing. I am many things. I am water. This is my dance through our world." This book explains the water cycle using a first-person narrative.

Try This! After reading the book, encourage children to talk about places where they can find water in their homes, in the school, and in the neighborhood.

Try This, Too! Use this book as a springboard for discussing lakes, rivers, and clouds. Ask children to draw their own illustrations modeled after Locker's depictions of various parts of the water cycle.